SMARTPHONES

by Tammy Gagne

Cody Koala
An Imprint of Pop!
popbooksonline.com

abdopublishing.com

Published by Pop!, a division of ABDO, PO Box 398166, Minneapolis, Minnesota 55439. Copyright © 2019 by POP, LLC. International copyrights reserved in all countries. No part of this book may be reproduced in any form without written permission from the publisher. Pop!™ is a trademark and logo of POP, LLC.

Printed in the United States of America, North Mankato, Minnesota

042018
092018

THIS BOOK CONTAINS
RECYCLED MATERIALS

Cover Photo: Shutterstock Images
Interior Photos: Shutterstock Images, 1, 5 (top), 5 (bottom left), 5 (bottom right), 9, 10, 13 (bottom right), 14, 16; iStockphoto, 6, 13 (top), 13 (bottom left), 19, 21

Editor: Charly Haley
Series Designer: Laura Mitchell

Library of Congress Control Number: 2017963468
Publisher's Cataloging-in-Publication Data

Names: Gagne, Tammy, author.
Title: Smartphones / by Tammy Gagne.
Description: Minneapolis, Minnesota : Pop!, 2019. | Series: 21st century inventions | Includes online resources and index.
Identifiers: ISBN 9781532160431 (lib.bdg.) | ISBN 9781532161551 (ebook) |
Subjects: LCSH: Smartphones--Juvenile literature. | Technological innovations--Juvenile literature. | Inventions--History--Juvenile literature. | Technology--History--Juvenile literature.
Classification: DDC 609--dc23

Cody Koala

Pop open this book and you'll find QR codes like this one, loaded with information, so you can learn even more!

Scan this code* and others like it while you read, or visit the website below to make this book pop.

popbooksonline.com/smartphones

*Scanning QR codes requires a web-enabled smart device with a QR code reader app and a camera.

Table of Contents

Chapter 1

What Are Smartphones?

Smartphones do a lot more than make calls. They take photos. They use the Internet. They send emails and text messages.

Watch a video here!

People used to use different machines to do those things. But now, smartphones do the jobs of phones, cameras, computers, and more.

The first smartphone was released in 1994.

Chapter 2

How Smartphones Work

Smartphones use **cell networks** to send text, photos, or videos. The networks have towers that send **data** between phones.

Learn more here!

Parts of a Smartphone

camera

speaker

battery charging

wireless Internet signal

touchscreen

apps

Smartphones work like small computers. But smartphones have **touchscreens**. People touch the screens with their fingers to type words or click on websites.

Smartphones are powered by batteries. They need to be plugged in to recharge.

Chapter 3

Using Smartphones

Old telephones and computers had to always be plugged in to be used. But smartphones can be used almost anywhere.

Learn more here!

Order your food
online now!

24|7   30'

Who delivers in
your neighborhood?

Find your favourite restaurant
More than 3,000 restaurants to choose

Special offers
Find the best deals

Smartphones give people news and weather reports. People shop online and order food from their phones. Smartphones are used as alarm clocks.

Most people use **apps** on their smartphones. Apps let people do specific things. There are millions of different apps. Some are games. Some are for reading or listening to music.

Chapter 4

The Future of Smartphones

Companies are working to make smartphones that can do even more things. Future phones may have better batteries. They won't need to be charged often.

Complete an activity here!

As **technology** improves, smartphones will become better and better.

It's expected that future smartphones will be able to download a full movie in just seconds instead of minutes.

Making Connections

Text-to-Self

Do you or your family members use smartphones? What do you use them for?

Text-to-Text

Have you read another book about smartphones or other new technology? What did you learn from that book?

Text-to-World

How has the world changed because of smartphones?

Glossary

app – a program that lets people do many different things on smartphones.

cell network – a system of towers that transmit information.

data – items of information.

technology – objects created by using science.

Index

Online Resources

popbooksonline.com

Thanks for reading this Cody Koala book!

Scan this code* and others like it in this book, or visit the website below to make this book pop!

popbooksonline.com/smartphones

*Scanning QR codes requires a web-enabled smart device with a QR code reader app and a camera.